HOW TO USE VI & INDEX MATCH EXCEL FUNCTIONS

DETAILED STEP BY STEP PRACTICAL EXPERIENCE GUIDE FOR ACCOUNTANTS

STERLING LIBS

Level 33, 25 Canada Square,

Canary Wharf, London E14 5LQ

resource@sterlinglibs.com

www.sterlinglibs.com

Copyright © 2016 by Sterling Libs

Straight Street Publishing

Editions ISBNs

Softcover

978-1-911037-06-4

Contents

Note to the reader

For most Excel users, VLOOKUP is the first complex formula they learn. Performing a lookup is an extremely valuable function for any situation where you're dealing with large data sets.

The first step to learning VLOOKUP is knowing when to use it.

In its most common usage, VLOOKUP is a database function, meaning that it works with database tables – or more simply, lists of things in an Excel worksheet. What sort of things? Well, any sort of thing. You may have a worksheet that contains a list of employees, or products, or customers, or CDs in your CD collection, or stars in the night sky. It doesn't really matter.

The function is used when you want to find a value in the left-hand column of a vertical array of data, and return the corresponding value from another column in the same array.

Another lookup function we will deal with is called INDEX MATCH which is more superior to VLOOKUP but not widely used by most excel basic users.

So you will get the benefit of learning both of these excel lookup functions and this is from the eye of an accountant. All that I will be showing you is from accounting perspective. Of course you can use excel in a whole host of other different ways but as an accountant, I will use show you how to use this functions from an accountants perspective.

Sterling Libs FCCA – London UK.

Introduction to VLOOKUP

What is VLOOKUP?

Well, of course it's an Excel *function*. It is one of the lookup and reference functions in excel when you need to find things in a table or a range by row. For example, look up an employee's last name by her employee number, or find her phone number by looking up her last name (just like a telephone book).

I am going to illustrate how you can use the VLOOK function on the assumption that you already have a passing understanding of Excel functions, and can use basic functions such as SUM, AVERAGE, and TODAY. In its most common usage, VLOOKUP is a *database* function, meaning that it works with database tables – or more simply, *lists* of things in an Excel worksheet.

What sort of things? Well, *any* sort of thing. You may have a worksheet that contains a list of employees, or products, or customers, or CDs in your CD collection, or stars in the galaxy. It doesn't really matter.

The secret to VLOOKUP is to organise your data so that the value you look up (for example employee's last name) is to the left of the return value you want to find (employee's phone number).

Before we continue, let's first learn how to familiarise ourselves with the excel version.

Excel Version

This practical guide is based on Excel 2013 Microsoft windows 8 operating system. You'll discover how to confirm that your computer is running in these version in a few minutes.

If you are using an earlier operating system (for example windows XP) this practical course will be equally relevant, but you may notice small differences in the appearance of some of the screen shots you will see in this practical guide.

This practical guide is written purely for Excel 2013 and, due to huge changes in this version, will not be useful for earlier versions (97, 2000, 2002 and 2003)

Checking your program and operating system

- Start/open Excel on your computer

- Click the "**FILE**" button at the top left corner as illustrated in the figure below

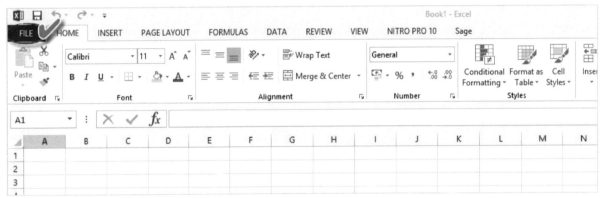

Fig. 1

- *After following the instruction above, a window similar to fig. 2 will appear*

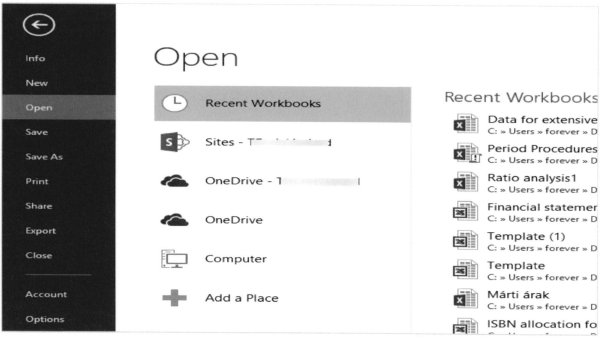

Fig. 2

- Follow the instructions illustrated in the figure below.

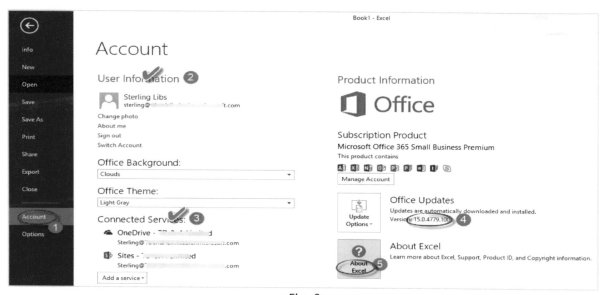

Fig. 3

1. Click the Account button at the bottom left as shown in the figure above

2. This shows the user information for the Microsoft account

3. *This shows the details of any Microsoft connected services this user has*

4. *This shows the version number of the Microsoft excel installed on your computer*

Checking the operating system

5. *Click the about button next to learn more about Microsoft excel, support & product ID details. A dialog is displayed with information about your copy of Excel. See below*

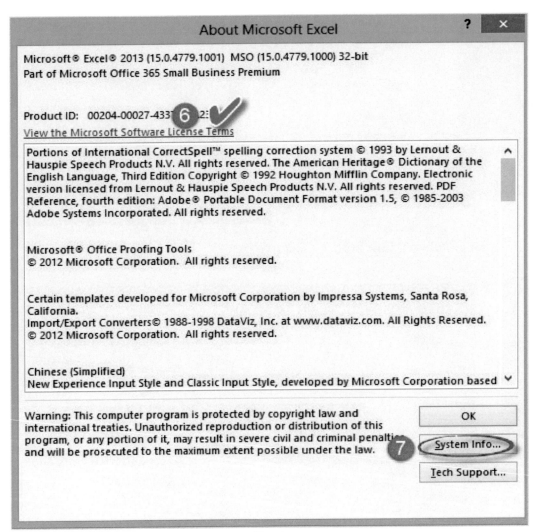

Fig. 4

6. *This is the product ID of your Microsoft excel that is installed on your computer*

7. *Click the system info....button. The operating system (OS) Name and version will then be visible at the top right of the dialog – See figure below*

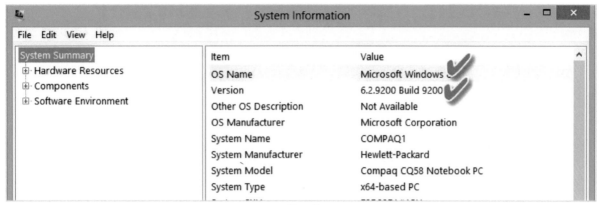

Fig. 5

- *Close the excel window – see illustration below (click x at the top right hand corner)*

Fig. 6

Getting started with VLOOKUP

Here's an example of a list, or database. In this case, it's a list of products that our fictitious company - Tristar stationers sells.

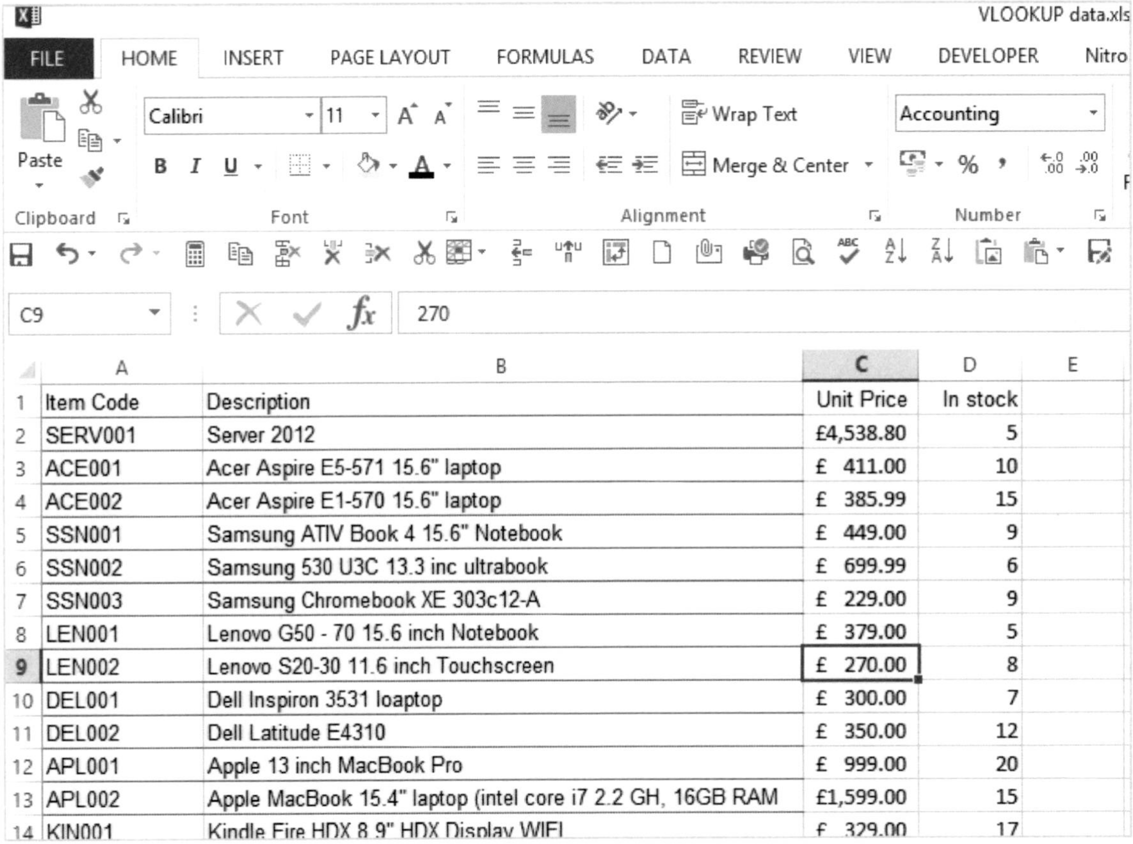

	A	B	C	D	E
1	Item Code	Description	Unit Price	In stock	
2	SERV001	Server 2012	£4,538.80	5	
3	ACE001	Acer Aspire E5-571 15.6" laptop	£ 411.00	10	
4	ACE002	Acer Aspire E1-570 15.6" laptop	£ 385.99	15	
5	SSN001	Samsung ATIV Book 4 15.6" Notebook	£ 449.00	9	
6	SSN002	Samsung 530 U3C 13.3 inc ultrabook	£ 699.99	6	
7	SSN003	Samsung Chromebook XE 303c12-A	£ 229.00	9	
8	LEN001	Lenovo G50 - 70 15.6 inch Notebook	£ 379.00	5	
9	LEN002	Lenovo S20-30 11.6 inch Touchscreen	£ 270.00	8	
10	DEL001	Dell Inspiron 3531 loaptop	£ 300.00	7	
11	DEL002	Dell Latitude E4310	£ 350.00	12	
12	APL001	Apple 13 inch MacBook Pro	£ 999.00	20	
13	APL002	Apple MacBook 15.4" laptop (intel core i7 2.2 GH, 16GB RAM	£1,599.00	15	
14	KIN001	Kindle Fire HDX 8.9" HDX Display WIFI	£ 329.00	17	

Fig. 7

Usually lists like this have some sort of unique identifier for each item in the list. In this case, the unique identifier is in the "Item Code" column.

Note: For the VLOOKUP function to work with a database/list, that list must have a column containing the unique identifier (or "key", or "ID"), and that column must be the first column in the table. Our sample database above satisfies this criterion.

The hardest part of using VLOOKUP is understanding exactly what it's for. So let's see if we can get that clear first:

VLOOKUP retrieves information from a database/list based on a supplied instance of the unique identifier.

Put another way, if you put the VLOOKUP function into a cell and pass it one of the unique identifiers from your database, it will return you one of the pieces of information associated with that unique identifier. In the example above, you would pass VLOOKUP an item code, and it would return to you either the corresponding item's description, its price, or its availability (its "In stock" quantity). Which of these pieces of information will it pass you back? Well, you get to decide this when you're creating the formula.

If all you need is one piece of information from the database, it would be a lot of trouble to go to construct a formula with a VLOOKUP function in it. Typically you would use this sort of functionality in a reusable spreadsheet, such as a template. Each time someone enters a valid item code, the system would retrieve all the necessary information about the corresponding item.

Let's create an example of this: An Invoice Template that we can reuse over and over in our fictitious company.

First we start Excel…

Fig. 8

… and we create ourselves a blank invoice: see figure below (you will have to create one from scratch). Make sure you resize cell B11 to make it a bit long and also make sure that you wrap text in it as illustrated in the figure below and do the same for cells B12-B19.

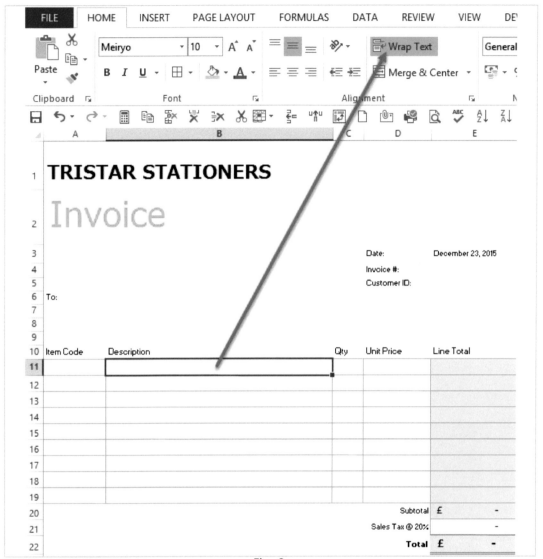

Fig. 9

Let's put some formulas in this invoice to help automate some tasks later.

In Cell E3, type in =NOW( ) or =TODAY( ) and then enter.

In cell E11, type in =C11*D11 and the press Enter.

10	Item Code	Description	Qty	Unit Price	Line Total
11					=C11*D11
12					

Fig. 10

Incorporating "IF" & "ISBLANK" functions

Once you press Enter, you will see something similar to "0.00" if you have formatted the cell to 2 decimal places or you will simply see "0" in cell E11.

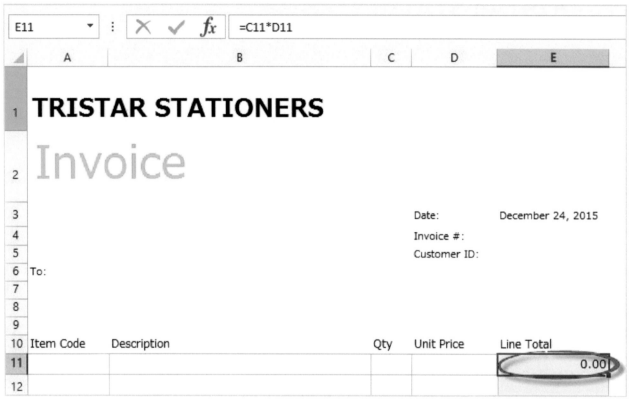

Fig. 11

Now, if you want to keep your invoice template tidy and don't want to see the 0.00 or the – sign on cell E11 if there are no figures in cell C11 and or D11, you can use "ISBLANK" & "IF" function. Do this, in cell E11, type in =IF(ISBLANK(C11),"",(C11*D11)). Another formula to use would be: =IF(C11="","",(C11*D11))

What you are basically saying here is this *"if cell C11 is blank, put nothing in cell E11, otherwise if there is something in cell C11, then multiply that with what is in cell D11.*

Let's try it and see,

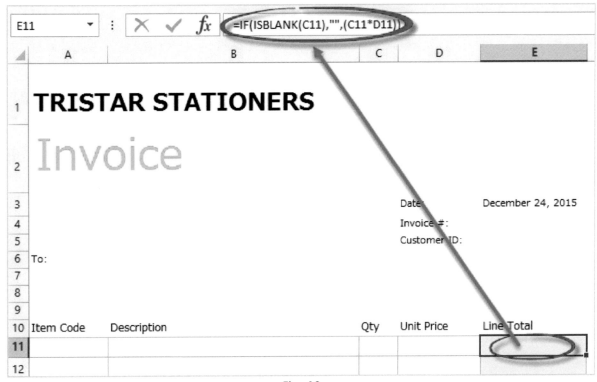

Fig. 12

Wala! The "0.00" and or "-", or "0"are gone from cell E11 because of the ISBLANK and IF function.

Click on the bottom right corner of cell E11 when you hoover over it and see the dark + sign. Now drag the click down up to cell E19 and release it – that will copy the formula to cell E12-E19.

Format cells E20 - E22 to show £ sign and in cell E20 type in the formula =SUM(E11:E19) and press enter, in cell E21 type in =E20*20% and press enter, and in cell E22 type in = SUM(E20:E21) and press enter.

You are now going to start using the VLOOKUP function!

The way this is going to work is this: You are going to fill the invoice template you have just created with a series of item codes in column "A" – starting from "A11", and the system will retrieve each item's description and price, which will be used to calculate the line total for each item (assuming we enter a valid quantity).

For the purposes of keeping this example simple, we will locate the product database on a separate sheet in the same workbook.

In reality, it's more likely that the product database would be located in a separate workbook. It makes little difference to the VLOOKUP function, which doesn't really care if the database is located on the same sheet, a different sheet, or a completely different workbook.

Now, open a new worksheet (call it *Product Database*) in the same workbook you have the blank invoice template and in cell A1- type in *"Item Code"* in cell B1- type in *Description"* in cell C1 – type in *Unit price"* and in cell D1 – type in – *"In stock"* (See figure below)

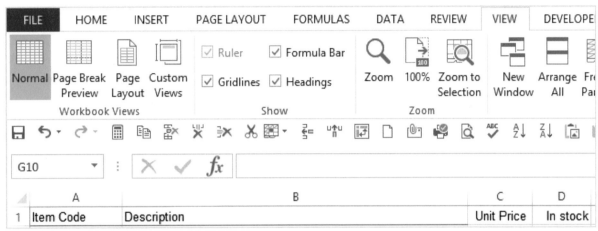

Fig. 13

Now fill in the worksheet from cell A2 – D25 as shown in fig. 14.

	A	B	C	D
1	Item Code	Description	Unit Price	In stock
2	SERV001	Server 2012	£4,538.80	5
3	ACE001	Acer Aspire E5-571 15.6" laptop	£ 411.00	10
4	ACE002	Acer Aspire E1-570 15.6" laptop	£ 385.99	15
5	SSN001	Samsung ATIV Book 4 15.6" Notebook	£ 449.00	9
6	SSN002	Samsung 530 U3C 13.3 inc ultrabook	£ 699.99	6
7	SSN003	Samsung Chromebook XE 303c12-A	£ 229.00	9
8	LEN001	Lenovo G50 - 70 15.6 inch Notebook	£ 379.00	5
9	LEN002	Lenovo S20-30 11.6 inch Touchscreen	£ 270.00	8
10	DEL001	Dell Inspiron 3531 loaptop	£ 300.00	7
11	DEL002	Dell Latitude E4310	£ 350.00	12
12	APL001	Apple 13 inch MacBook Pro	£ 999.00	20
13	APL002	Apple MacBook 15.4" laptop (intel core i7 2.2 GH, 16GB RAM	£1,599.00	15
14	KIN001	Kindle Fire HDX 8.9" HDX Display WIFI	£ 329.00	17
15	SST001	Samsung Galaxy Tab 4.10 inch Tablet (Black)	£ 294.56	10
16	SST002	Samsung Galaxy Tab S 10.5" Titanium Bronze Tablet	£ 322.00	11
17	API001	Apple ipad Air 2 16GB WIFI space grey	£ 349.00	30
18	API002	Apple ipad mini (7.9 inch multi - touch) Tablet PC 32GB WIFI	£ 425.25	13
19	CAN001	Canon EOS Digital SLR Camera (EF-S 18.55 cm f/3.5)	£ 749.00	15
20	CAN002	Canon Poershot SX700 HS Zoom	£ 320.00	25
21	CAN003	Canon SX60 HS Power shot Digital Camera	£ 429.65	22
22	NIK001	Nikon D3200 Digital SLR Camera with 18.55mm VR lens kit	£ 649.99	7
23	NIK002	Nikon D5000 Digital SLR Camera with 18-55 mm VR lens kit	£ 499.99	9
24	PAN001	Panasonic PTA 6000E LCD projector - 3D	£1,999.00	3
25	LG001	LGPA70G Portable WXGALED Projector	£ 514.80	5
26	EPS001	Epson EH-TW5100 Full HD 1080p 3D Home cinema & gaming	£ 615.25	7
27	LG002	LGPF80G Full HD LED projector	£1,078.80	8
28	BEN001	BenQ W1200 DLP Projector	£ 736.38	5
29	VIE001	Viewsonic PLED-W800 DLP Projector	£ 495.67	9

Fig. 14

Now, select the data range from A2-D29 and name it Product. Type the word Product to replace the text A2 in the area shown by a green tick in fig. 15.

	Product ✓ ▾	:	✕ ✓	fx	SERV001		

	A	B	C	D
2	SERV001	Server 2012	£4,538.80	5
3	ACE001	Acer Aspire E5-571 15.6" laptop	£ 411.00	10
4	ACE002	Acer Aspire E1-570 15.6" laptop	£ 385.99	15
5	SSN001	Samsung ATIV Book 4 15.6" Notebook	£ 449.00	9
6	SSN002	Samsung 530 U3C 13.3 inc ultrabook	£ 699.99	6
7	SSN003	Samsung Chromebook XE 303c12-A	£ 229.00	9
8	LEN001	Lenovo G50 - 70 15.6 inch Notebook	£ 379.00	5
9	LEN002	Lenovo S20-30 11.6 inch Touchscreen	£ 270.00	8
10	DEL001	Dell Inspiron 3531 loaptop	£ 300.00	7
11	DEL002	Dell Latitude E4310	£ 350.00	12
12	APL001	Apple 13 inch MacBook Pro	£ 999.00	20
13	APL002	Apple MacBook 15.4" laptop (intel core i7 2.2 GH, 16GB RAM	£1,599.00	15
14	KIN001	Kindle Fire HDX 8.9" HDX Display WIFI	£ 329.00	17
15	SST001	Samsung Galaxy Tab 4.10 inch Tablet (Black)	£ 294.56	10
16	SST002	Samsung Galaxy Tab S 10.5" Titanium Bronze Tablet	£ 322.00	11
17	API001	Apple ipad Air 2 16GB WIFI space grey	£ 349.00	30
18	API002	Apple ipad mini (7.9 inch multi - touch) Tablet PC 32GB WIFI	£ 425.25	13
19	CAN001	Canon EOS Digital SLR Camera (EF-S 18.55 cm f/3.5)	£ 749.00	15
20	CAN002	Canon Poershot SX700 HS Zoom	£ 320.00	25
21	CAN003	Canon SX60 HS Power shot Digital Camera	£ 429.65	22
22	NIK001	Nikon D3200 Digital SLR Camera with 18.55mm VR lens kit	£ 649.99	7
23	NIK002	Nikon D5000 Digital SLR Camera with 18-55 mm VR lens kit	£ 499.99	9
24	PAN001	Panasonic PTA 6000E LCD projector - 3D	£1,999.00	3
25	LG001	LGPA70G Portable WXGALED Projector	£ 514.80	5
26	EPS001	Epson EH-TW5100 Full HD 1080p 3D Home cinema & gaming	£ 615.25	7
27	LG002	LGPF80G Full HD LED projector	£1,078.80	8
28	BEN001	BenQ W1200 DLP Projector	£ 736.38	5
29	VIE001	Viewsonic PLED-W800 DLP Projector	£ 495.67	9

Fig. 15

Okay,

Open another new worksheet in the same workbook (name it Customer List) and write down the following list of customers.

Here is how it should look like in your excel sheet when you are done - see fig. 95.

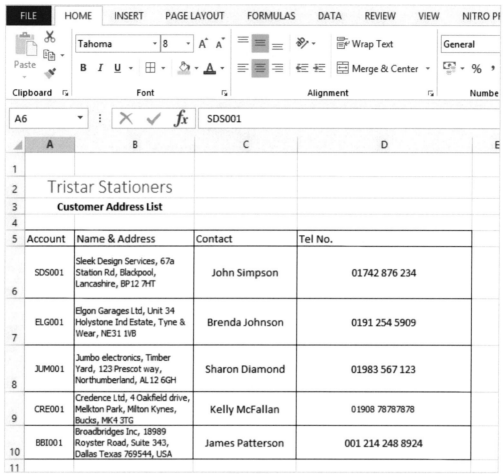

Fig. 16

Now highlight cell A6-D10 and name that range Customer. We will use it later.

Using the VLOOKUP formula/function

Okay,

In order to test the VLOOKUP formula we're about to write, we first enter a valid item code into cell

	Item Code	Description		Qty	Unit Price	Line Total
9						
10	Item Code	Description		Qty	Unit Price	Line Total
11	SERV001					
12						

Fig. 17

A11 of the blank invoice template we created earlier on.

Next, we move the active cell to the cell in which we want information retrieved from the database by VLOOKUP to be stored. Interestingly, this is the step that most people get wrong. To explain further: We are about to create a VLOOKUP formula that will retrieve the description that corresponds to the item code in cell A11. Where do we want this description put when we get it? In cell B11, of course. So that's where we write the VLOOKUP formula – in cell B11.

Select cell B11.

We need to locate the VLOOKUP function and get some assistance in completing it. Follow steps 1-3 as illustrated in the figure below.

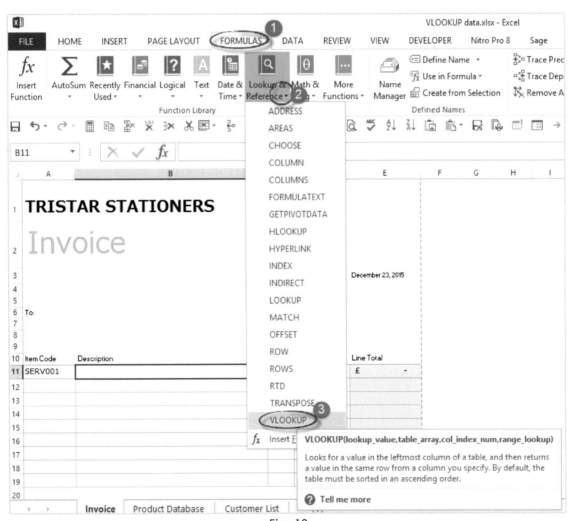

Fig. 18

VLOOKUP Function Arguments

After step 3 as illustrated in the figure above, The **Function Arguments** box appears, prompting us for all the *arguments* (or *parameters*) needed in order to complete the VLOOKUP function. You can think of this box as the function is asking us the following questions:

1. *What unique identifier are you looking up in the database?*

2. *Where is the database?*

3. *Which piece of information from the database, associated with the unique identifier, do you wish to have retrieved for you?*

The first three arguments are shown in bold, indicating that they are mandatory arguments (the VLOOKUP function is incomplete without them and will not return a valid value). The fourth argument is not bold, meaning that it's optional.

See figure below.

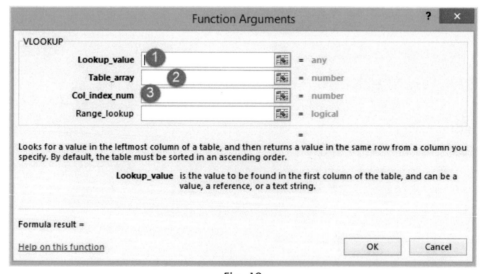

Fig. 19

We will complete the arguments in order, top to bottom.

The first argument we need to complete is the **Lookup value** argument. The function needs us to tell it where to find the unique identifier (the *item code* in this case) that it should be retuning the description of. We must select the item code we entered earlier (in A11).

Click on the selector icon to the right of the first argument.

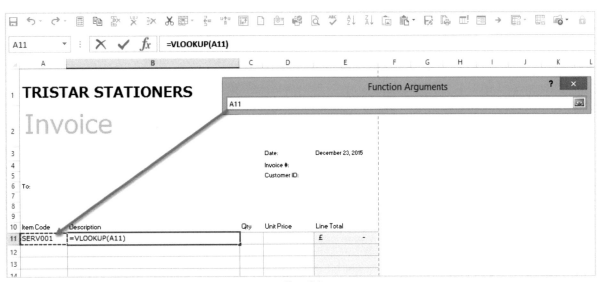

Fig. 20

Then click once on the cell containing the item code (A11), and press **Enter**.

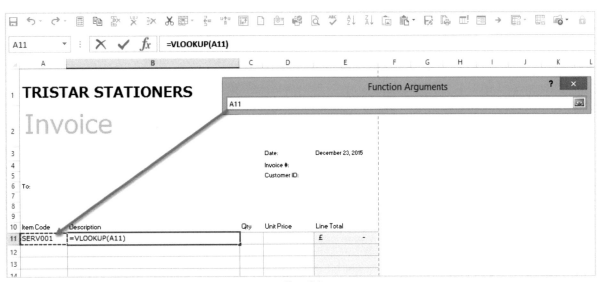

Fig. 21

The value of "A11" is inserted into the first argument.

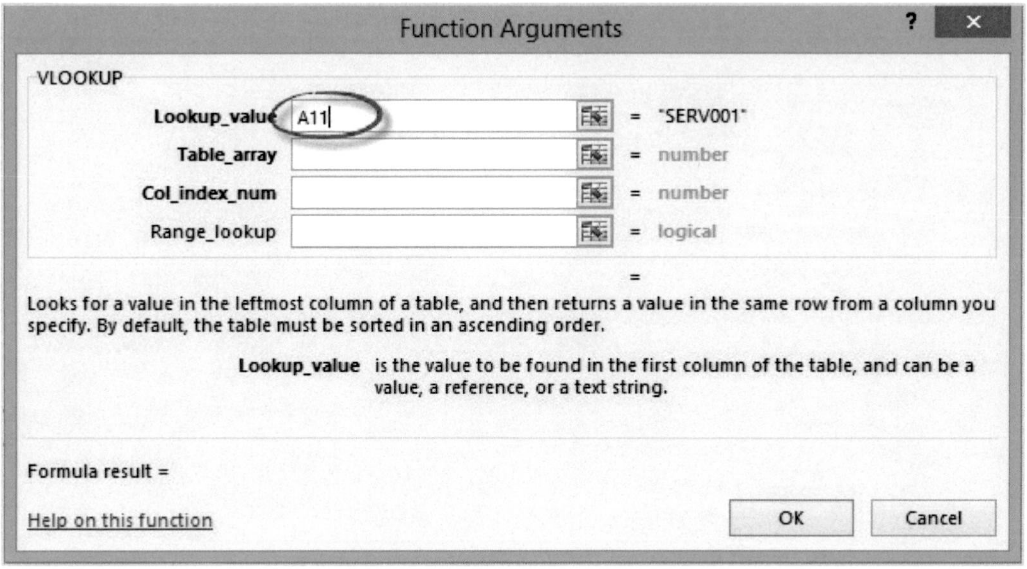

Fig. 22

Now we need to enter a value for the **Table_array** argument. In other words, we need to tell VLOOKUP where to find the database/list. Click on the Table _array box and type in Product (Do you remember we named the Product database range – Product? that is why we are typing the word Product here). We are basically telling VLOOKUP that the database is called product.

See figure below.

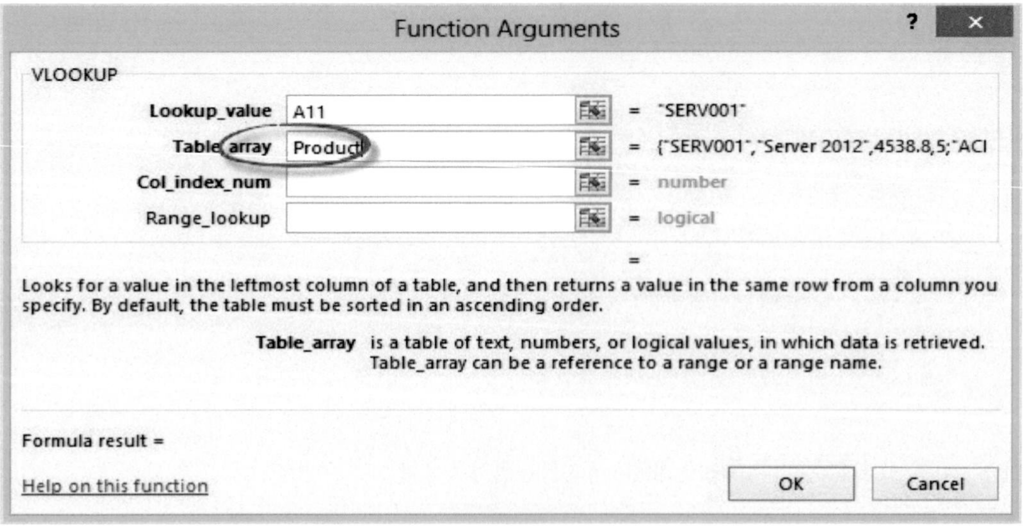

Fig. 23

Now we need to enter the third argument, **Col_index_num**. We use this argument to specify to VLOOKUP which piece of information from the database, associate with our item code in A11, we wish to have returned to us. In this particular example, we wish to have the item's description returned to us. If you look on the database worksheet, you'll notice that the "Description" column is the second column in the database. This means that we must enter a value of "2" into the **Col_index_num** box: see figure below.

Fig. 24

It is important to note that that we are not entering a "2" here because the "Description" column is in the **B** column on that worksheet. If the database happened to start in column **K** of the worksheet, we would still enter a "2" in this field.

Finally, we need to decide whether to enter a value into the final VLOOKUP argument, **Range_lookup**. This argument requires either a **true** or **false** value, or it should be left blank. When using VLOOKUP with databases (as is true 90% of the time), then the way to decide what to put in this argument can be thought of as follows:

If the first column of the database (the column that contains the unique identifiers) is sorted alphabetically/numerically in ascending order, then it's possible to enter a value of **true** into this argument, or leave it blank.

If the first column of the database is not sorted, or it's sorted in descending order, then you must enter a value of **false** into this argument.

As the first column of our database is not sorted, we enter **false** into this argument.

That's it! We've entered all the information required for VLOOKUP to return the value we need. Click the **OK** button.

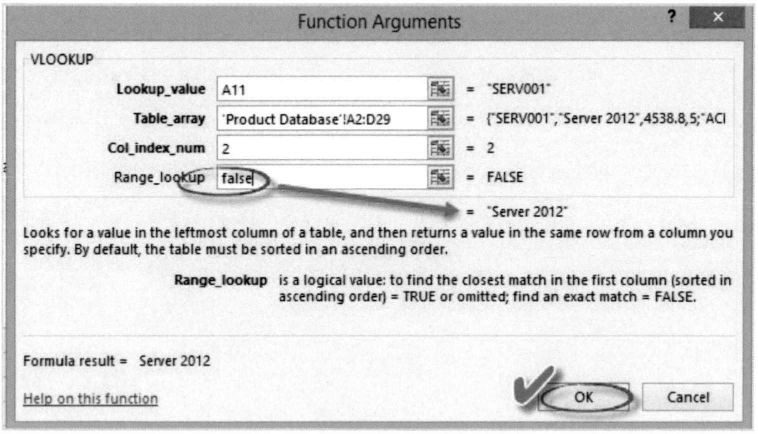

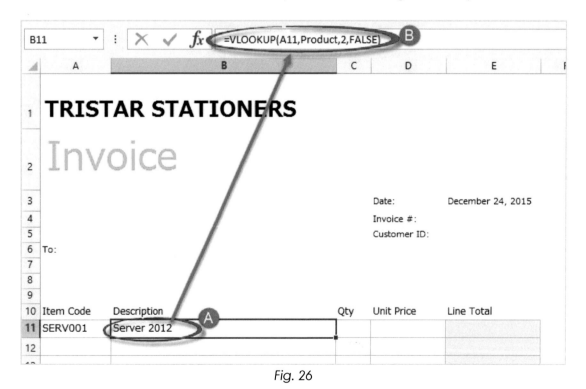

Fig. 25

Notice that after you click OK as illustrated in the figure above, the description corresponding to item code "SERV001" has been correctly entered into cell B11 (illustrated by letter "A" in the figure below of which the full VLOOKUP formula is illustrated by letter "B" in the figure below).

Fig. 26

We can perform a similar set of steps to get the item's price returned into cell D11. Note that the new formula must be created in cell D11. The result will look like this:

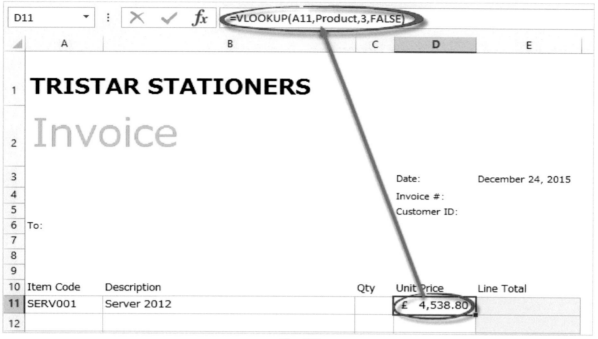

Fig. 27

Use the "ISBLANK" and "IF" function in cells B11 & D1. This is to avaid the #N/A signs in cell B11 & D11 should there be no value in A11.

Here is how the formulas should look like;

B11- =IF(ISBLANK(A11),"",VLOOKUP(A11,2,FALSE)) or =IF(A11="","",VLOOKUP(A11,**2**,FALSE))

D11- = IF(ISBLANK(A11),"",VLOOKUP(A11,3,FALSE)) or =IF(A11="","",VLOOKUP(A11,**3**,FALSE))

Note that the only difference between the two formulas is that the third argument (**Col_index_num**) has changed from a "2" to a "3" for formula in D11 (because we want data retrieved from the 3rd column in the database for the case of the unit price of the product code in A11).

Now copy the formula in B11 to B12-B19. To do this select cell B11, then hoover the mouse at the bottom right corner of cell B11 till you see the dark **+** , once you see it, click and hold at the bottom right side of cell B11 and drag your mouse down to cell B19 then release it.

Do the same for formula in D11.

See fig. 28.

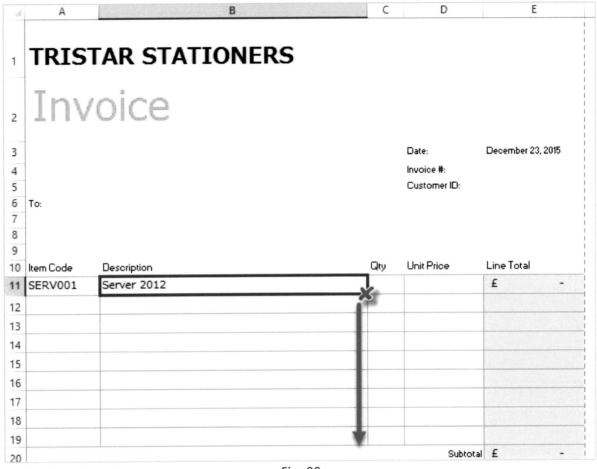

Fig. 28

Now, if we enter a different item code into cell A11, we will begin to see the power of the VLOOKUP function: The description cell changes to match the new item code.

First, let's put a drop down list for all the products into cell A11 – A19. To do this, left click to select cell A11, then hold the click and drag your mouse down until you reach cell A19, then release the click – You have now selected cell A11-A19.

Incorporating Data Validation

Select Data>Data validation>Data Validation again. See fig. 29.

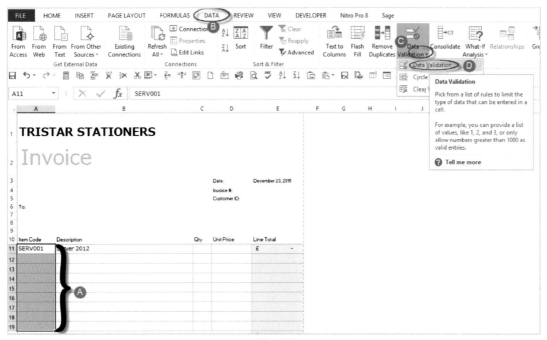

Fig. 29

Once you select Data validation (step D as illustrated in the figure above) a window similar to the figure below will appear.

Fig. 30

Click on the drop down arrow and select "List".

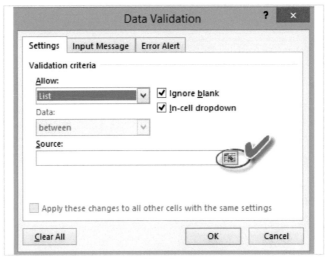

Fig. 31

Now click on the selector icon to the right of source then select the product database sheet and then select cell A2 – A29 and press Enter. See figure below.

	A	B	C	D	E	F	G	H	I	J
1	Item Code	Description	Unit Price	In stock						
2	SERV001	Server 2012	£4				Data Validation	?	×	
3	ACE001	Acer Aspire E5-571 15.6" laptop	£							
4	ACE002	Acer Aspire E1-570 15.6" laptop	£		='Product Database'!$A$2:$A$29					
5	SSN001	Samsung ATIV Book 4 15.6" Notebook	£ 449.00	9						
6	SSN002	Samsung 530 U3C 13.3 inc ultrabook	£ 699.99	6						
7	SSN003	Samsung Chromebook XE 303c12-A	£ 229.00	9						
8	LEN001	Lenovo G50 - 70 15.6 inch Notebook	£ 379.00	5						
9	LEN002	Lenovo S20-30 11.6 inch Touchscreen	£ 270.00	8						
10	DEL001	Dell Inspiron 3531 loaptop	£ 300.00	7						
11	DEL002	Dell Latitude E4310	£ 350.00	12						
12	APL001	Apple 13 inch MacBook Pro	£ 999.00	20						
13	APL002	Apple MacBook 15.4" laptop (intel core i7 2.2 GH, 16GB RA	£1,599.00	15						
14	KIN001	Kindle Fire HDX 8.9" HDX Display WIFI	£ 329.00	17						
15	SST001	Samsung Galaxy Tab 4.10 inch Tablet (Black)	£ 294.56	10						
16	SST002	Samsung Galaxy Tab S 10.5" Titanium Bronze Tablet	£ 322.00	11						
17	API001	Apple ipad Air 2 16GB WIFI space grey	£ 349.00	30						
18	API	Apple ipad mini (7.9 inch multi - touch) Tablet PC 32GB WIFI	£ 425.25	13						
19	CAN001	Canon EOS Digital SLR Camera (EF-S 18.55 cm f3.5)	£ 749.00	15						
20	CAN002	Canon Poershot SX700 HS Zoom	£ 320.00	25						
21	CAN003	Canon SX60 HS Power shot Digital Camera	£ 429.65	22						
22	NIK001	Nikon D3200 Digital SLR Camera with 18.55 mm VR lens kit	£ 649.99	7						
23	NIK002	Nikon D5000 Digital SLR Camera with 18-55 mm VR lens kit	£ 499.99	9						
24	PAN001	Panasonic PTA 6000E LCD projector - 3	£1,999.00	3						
25	LG001	LGPA70G Portable WXGALED Projector	£ 514.80	5						
26	EPS001	Epson EH-TW5100 Full HD 1080p 3D Home cinema & gaming	£ 615.25	7						

Invoice   Product Database   Customer List

Fig. 32

After you press Enter, this is what you will see;

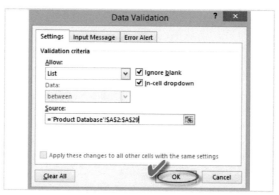

Fig. 33

Click OK.

You can now select any of the product codes from cell A11 – A19, see below illustrated by drop down arrow in "A" and products in "B".

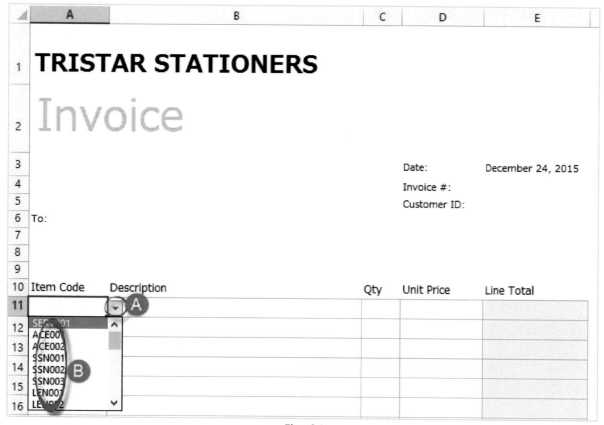

Fig. 34

Let's complete this invoice template by automating the input of the customer details once a customer account is selected.

Put a data validation for customer account numbers in cell E5.

Merge cells B6-B8, select the merged cell and click "Wrap Text", "Align left" and "Middle Align" – see figure below.

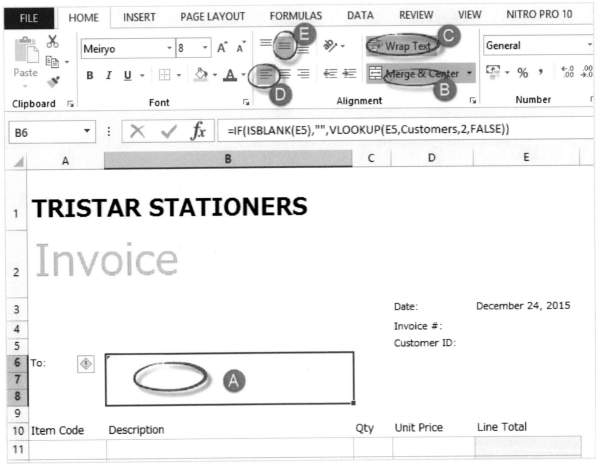

Fig. 35

Now put a VLOOKUP formula to the merged cells to return the customer address selected in cell E5.

Here is how the VLOOKUP function will look like.

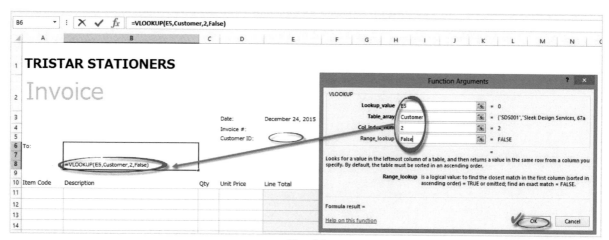

Fig. 36

Use "ISBLANK" and "IF" function as well in the merged cell to avoid #N/A error in case there is no value in cell E5. So the formula should look like this; =IF(ISBLANK(E5),"",VLOOKUP(E5,Customer,2,False)) or =IF(E5="","",VLOOKUP(E5,Customer,2,False)). Click on the merged cell B6-B8 and on the formula bar include the missing "IF" & "ISBLANK" function parts to VLOOKUP formula.

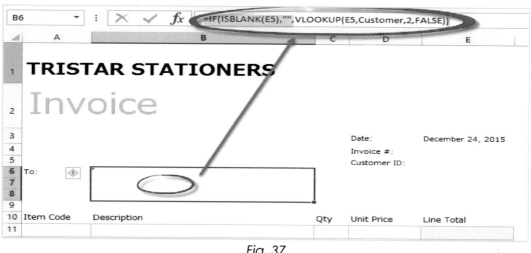

Fig. 37

Now let's test our work! I am quite excited now, wow!

Okay,

Here is a purchase order you have received from one of your customers;

Sleek Design Services

Purchase Order

Date: 24-Dec-15
PO # [100]

Supplier

Sales Manager
Tristar Stationers
55 Shelton Street
London, WC2H 9JQ
020 7836 1234

Deliver To

John Simpson
Sleek Design Services
67a Station Road Blackpool
Lancashire, BP12 7HT
01742876234

Shipping Method	Shipping Terms	Delivery Date
Standard	As per agreement	No later than 15 Jan 2016

Qty	Description	Unit Price	Line Total
1	Server 2012	£4,538.80	£4,538.80
5	Kindle Fire HDX 8.9" HDX Display WIFI	£329.00	£1,645.00
		Subtotal	£6,183.80
		Sales Tax@ 20%	£1,236.76
		Total	£7,420.56

Please send two copies of your invoice.

Enter this order in accordance with the prices, terms, delivery method, and specifications listed above.

Please notify us immediately if you are unable to ship as specified.

Send all correspondence to:

John Simpson
67a Station Road, Blackpool
Lancashire, BP12 7HT
Phone 0174286234
Fax 01742876000

Authorized by   Date

Automating tasks using VLOOKUP function

Now, let's raise an invoice for this customer using the invoice template you have just created using the VLOOKUP function. Make it invoice number 1234.

Select cell E5 (notice that you will see a drop down arrow) and select from the drop down list account code SDS001. Notice that the name and address of the customer appears on merged cells B6-B8 once you select the account code in cell E5.

Now select cell A11 and notice that a drop down arrow becomes visible. Click the drop down arrow and from the drop down list select SERV001 which is the code for the Server 2012. Notice that the product description- Server 2012 is automatically displayed on cell B11 and the unit price is automatically displayed on cell D11. Type in 1 on cell C11.

Select cell A12 and via the drop down list, select KIN001 and notice that in cell B12, "Kindle Fire HDX 8.9' Display WIFI" is automatically appears because of the VLOOKUP formula in Cell B12. Also notice that in cell D12 the price of £329.00 is automatically displayed because yet again, you have the VLOOKUP formula in cell D12.

And because the customer needs 5 of the Kindle Fire HDX, type in 5 in cell C12.

Here is how the final invoice looks like now:

Fig. 38

There you have it! VLOOKUP, done!

I hope you enjoyed that. I certainly did.

Next..... INDEX MATCH function

Introduction to INDEX MATCH excel function

When deciding between which vertical lookup formula to use, you will over time find that INDEX MATCH is a better formula than VLOOKUP.

The key difference between INDEX MATCH and VLOOKUP is that VLOOKUP requires a **static column reference** while INDEX MATCH uses a **dynamic column reference**.

With VLOOKUP, most people will input a specific, static number to indicate which column they want to return from but when you use INDEX MATCH, the formula allows you to manually choose which column you want to pull from.

The reason this leads to fewer errors is because when you follow the INDEX MATCH syntax, you click **directly** on the field containing the value you want to return.

With the VLOOKUP syntax, you specify your entire table array, **AND THEN** you specify a column reference to indicate which column you want to pull data from.

Use INDEX MATCH instead of VLOOKUP if you want to lookup data which is not in the first column, or you want to look to the left of the lookup data, rather than to the right (which is all VLOOKUP can do).

For many users, VLOOKUP just does what they need, just as we have used it in our previous example with the invoice. But there are three scenarios where VLOOKUP falls short and that's where INDEX MATCH could come in handy:

- *VLOOKUP can only look from left to right.*

    » You look a value in one column in a table/range, and then return a value from a column to the right.

    » But what happens if you want to look from right to left? VLOOKUP simply can't do that. INDEX MATCH can.

- *VLOOKUP is prone to error, especially in big spreadsheets*

    » With VLOOKUP, you specify a number to represent which column you want to return the value from. So you have count the columns to figure out which one you want. Hopefully you'll notice if you get it wrong but what if you don't? Finding and debugging this error can be a nightmare.

» With INDEX MATCH, you select the specific column of data from which you want to return the value. That's much more reliable and easier to debug when things go wrong.

- *VLOOKUP slows down big spreadsheets.*

  » When the value you are looking up is in one column, and the value you want to return is in the 50th column in the table/range, VLOOKUP requires you to select all 50 columns. This results in a lot of extra computations and can bring large spreadsheets to their knees.

  » With INDEX MATCH, you select the column containing the lookup value and the column containing the return value, and nothing else. That makes INDEX MATCH much more efficient.

Here is something I want you to do first before we continue,

Open (if it is not already open) the excel book that you created in the VLOOKUP example.

Select the invoice worksheet and delete all the VLOOKUP formulae from the invoice (formula in cells such as B11, D11, B12, D12 – just select those cells and press delete – assuming you have not protected them, if you have first unprotect them then delete the formula), leave the data validations as they are.

Select the product description sheet.

28	BEN001	BenQ W1200 DLP Projector	£ 736.38	5	
29	VIE001	Viewsonic PLED-W800 DLP Projector	£ 495.67	9	
30					
31					

Invoice   Product Database   Customer List   ⊕

READY

Fig. 39

Then highlight cell A2:A29 (letter A- as illustrated in the figure below) and name it *itemcode* (letter B- as illustrated in the figure below) - (all one word – do not to leave spaces).

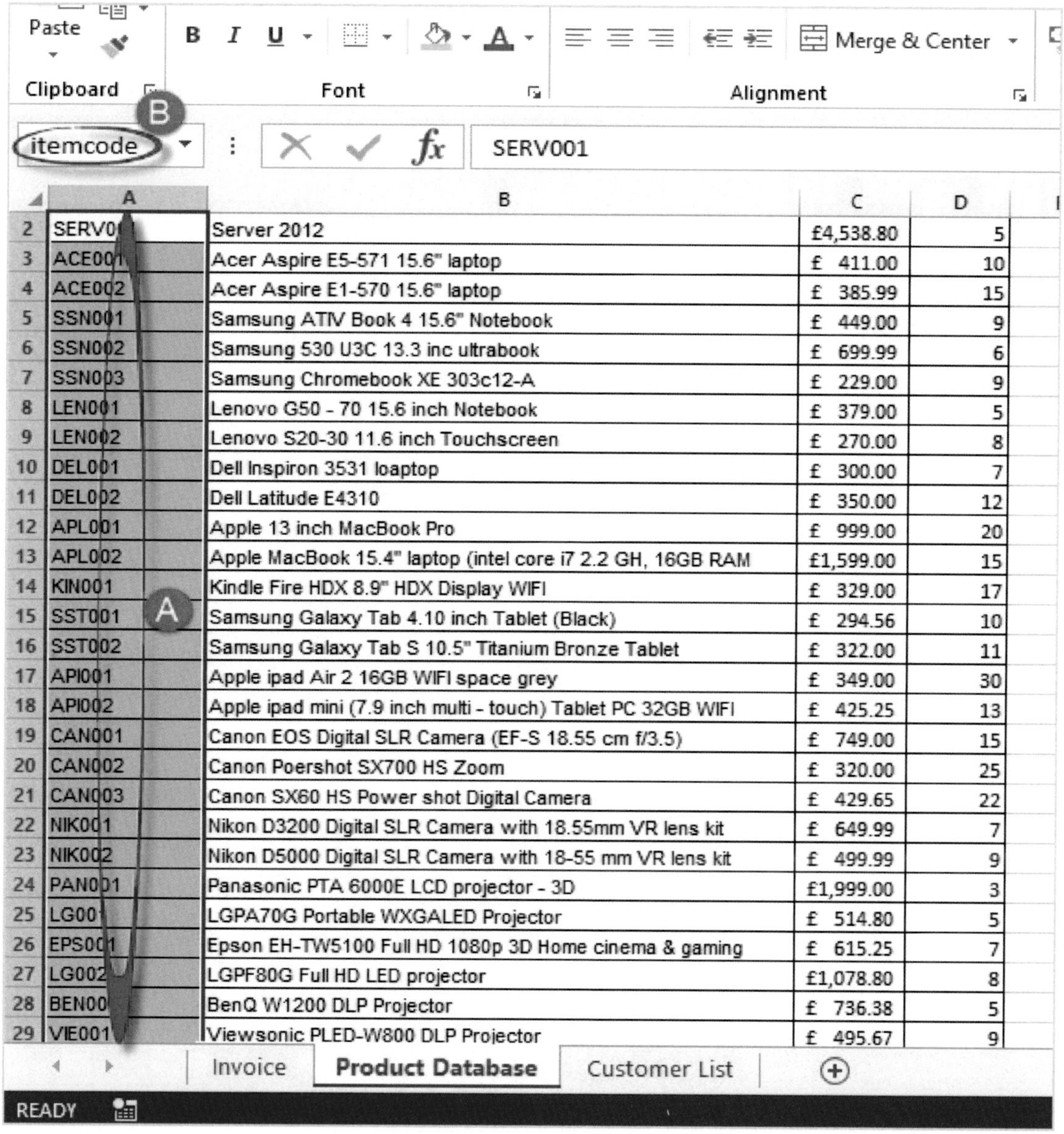

Fig. 40

Do the same thing for cell B2:B29 and name it *productdescription* and same thing to cell C2:C29 and name it *unitprice*. We will use this later as arrays in our INDEX MATCH formula.

Select the Customer List sheet;

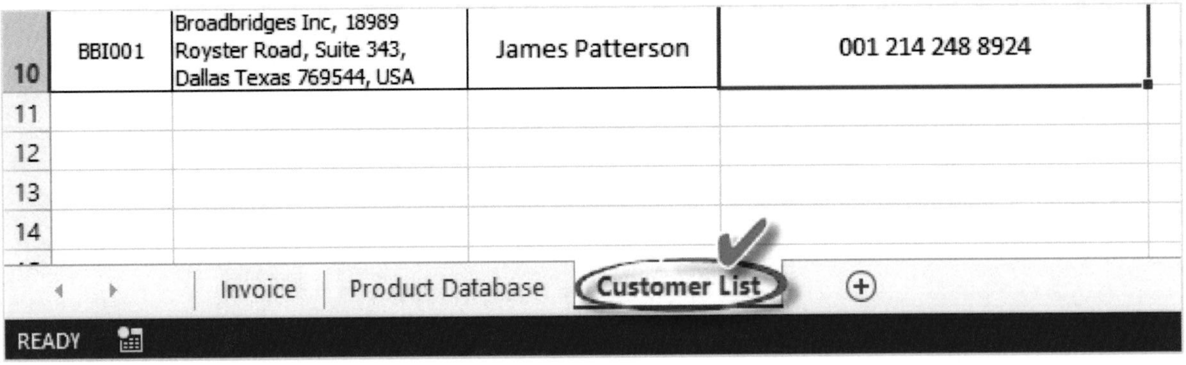

Fig. 41

Highlight cell A6:A10 (letter A- as illustrated in the figure below) and name it *Customeraccount* (letter B-as illustrated in the figure below).

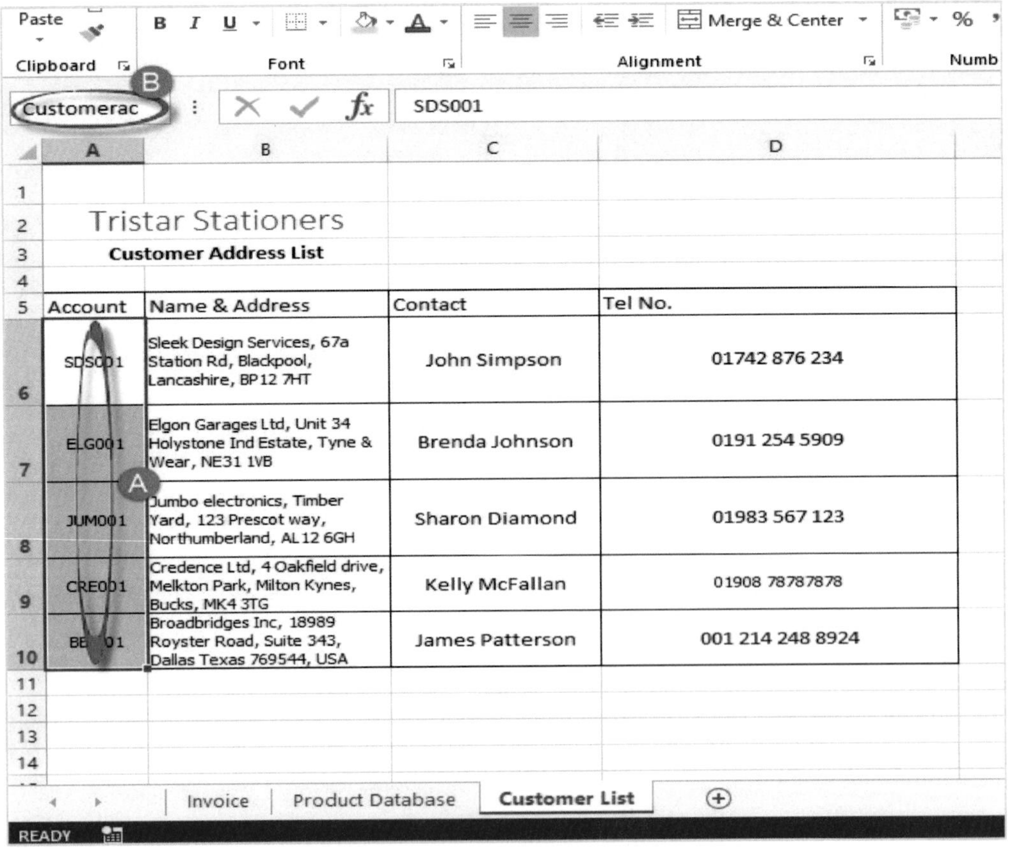

Fig. 42

Do the same for cell B6:B10 and name it *Custmeraddress.*

Now,

Let's put the INDEX MATCH formula to use.

But before we begin, we are going to first look at the INDEX function on its own and the MATCH function on its own then later look at them as "one" function.

INDEX function:

The basic INDEX function returns a **VALUE** based on a **defined array / column** and a **row number.** The syntax from Excel is as follows:

=INDEX(**array** , **row number**)

Example;

Select your product list worksheet from your workbook and in it we will try to find what price is on row number 11.

Here is how to do it – see figure below:

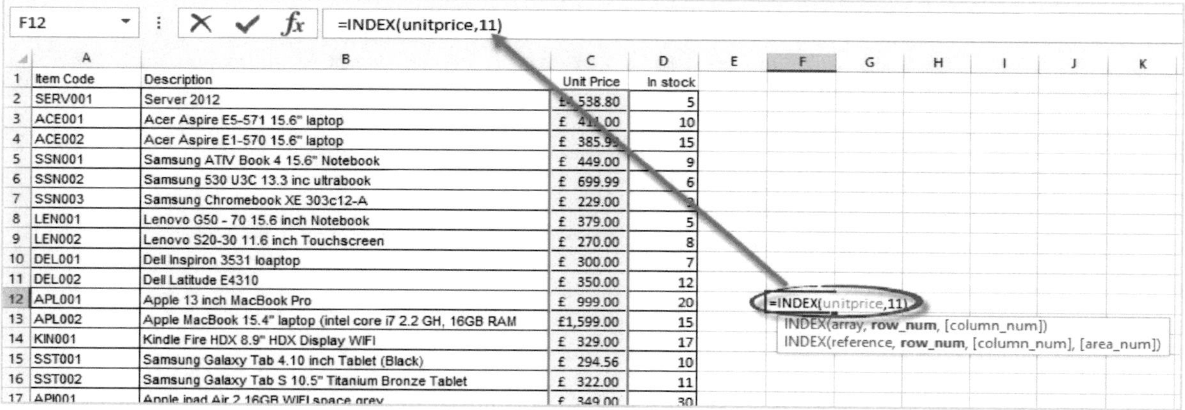

	A	B	C	D
1	Item Code	Description	Unit Price	In stock
2	SERV001	Server 2012	[illegible]538.80	5
3	ACE001	Acer Aspire E5-571 15.6" laptop	£ 4[illegible].00	10
4	ACE002	Acer Aspire E1-570 15.6" laptop	£ 385.9[illegible]	15
5	SSN001	Samsung ATIV Book 4 15.6" Notebook	£ 449.00	9
6	SSN002	Samsung 530 U3C 13.3 inc ultrabook	£ 699.99	6
7	SSN003	Samsung Chromebook XE 303c12-A	£ 229.00	[illegible]
8	LEN001	Lenovo G50 - 70 15.6 inch Notebook	£ 379.00	5
9	LEN002	Lenovo S20-30 11.6 inch Touchscreen	£ 270.00	8
10	DEL001	Dell Inspiron 3531 loaptop	£ 300.00	7
11	DEL002	Dell Latitude E4310	£ 350.00	12
12	APL001	Apple 13 inch MacBook Pro	£ 999.00	20
13	APL002	Apple MacBook 15.4" laptop (intel core i7 2.2 GH, 16GB RAM	£1,599.00	15
14	KIN001	Kindle Fire HDX 8.9" HDX Display WIFI	£ 329.00	17
15	SST001	Samsung Galaxy Tab 4.10 inch Tablet (Black)	£ 294.56	10
16	SST002	Samsung Galaxy Tab S 10.5" Titanium Bronze Tablet	£ 322.00	11
17	API001	Apple ipad Air 2 16GB WIFI space grey	£ 349.00	30

Fig. 43

This is what is happening here; you are telling the INDEX function to return you a value from an array called unitprice (remember we named this earlier on. If you want to see all the named ranges in your workbook, just click F3) and specifically from row number 11. Now, if you press the enter button, you should see the figure £999.00 as the value returned and indeed if you count from the top under the heading unit price, the 11th value is £999.00.

The MATCH function

The basic MATCH function returns a **NUMBER** based on the relative position of a **lookup value** within a **defined array / column.**

The syntax from Excel is as follows: =MATCH(**lookup value** , **lookup array** , **match type**).

Here is an example – see figure below.

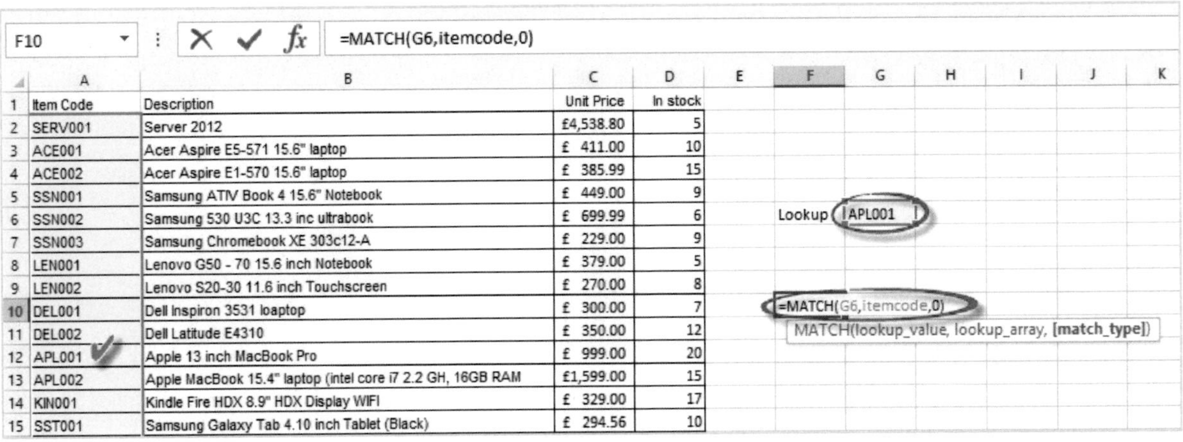

	A	B	C	D
1	Item Code	Description	Unit Price	In stock
2	SERV001	Server 2012	£4,538.80	5
3	ACE001	Acer Aspire E5-571 15.6" laptop	£ 411.00	10
4	ACE002	Acer Aspire E1-570 15.6" laptop	£ 385.99	15
5	SSN001	Samsung ATIV Book 4 15.6" Notebook	£ 449.00	9
6	SSN002	Samsung 530 U3C 13.3 inc ultrabook	£ 699.99	6
7	SSN003	Samsung Chromebook XE 303c12-A	£ 229.00	9
8	LEN001	Lenovo G50 - 70 15.6 inch Notebook	£ 379.00	5
9	LEN002	Lenovo S20-30 11.6 inch Touchscreen	£ 270.00	8
10	DEL001	Dell Inspiron 3531 loaptop	£ 300.00	7
11	DEL002	Dell Latitude E4310	£ 350.00	12
12	APL001	Apple 13 inch MacBook Pro	£ 999.00	20
13	APL002	Apple MacBook 15.4" laptop (intel core i7 2.2 GH, 16GB RAM	£1,599.00	15
14	KIN001	Kindle Fire HDX 8.9" HDX Display WIFI	£ 329.00	17
15	SST001	Samsung Galaxy Tab 4.10 inch Tablet (Black)	£ 294.56	10

Fig. 44

This is what is happening here.

You are telling the MATCH function to look up APL001 from the *itemcode* named range (remember we named this range earlier) and the number zero in the MATCH formula is telling it to look for the exact match to APL001 then return its relative position. In this case when you press enter from your keyboard after closing the brackets in MATCH formula, you see that the relative position for APL001 is 11. This is actually true because if you count the position where APL001 is from the top of the item code heading from your product list worksheet, you will realise that APL001 is on row 11.

INDEX MATCH

When we combine both the INDEX formula and the MATCH formula, the number that the MATCH formula returns becomes the row number for your INDEX formula. To paraphrase the INDEX MATCH would be something like these: =INDEX(**array**,**MATCH formula**).

Below is an example of using the INDEX MATCH to return "Customer address" for our lookup value when using our invoice we created earlier on.

Here is what you are going to do;

i.   Select the invoice worksheet from your workbook.

ii. Click the drop down arrow on cell E5 and select ELG00.

iii. Now, select the merged cell B6:B8 and type in the INDEX MATCH formula – =INDEX(Customeraddress,MATCH(E5,Customeraccount,0)) – see figure below.

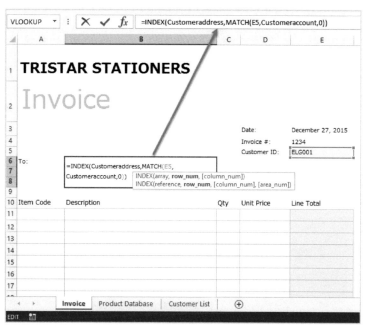

Fig. 45

This is what is happening here;

You are basically saying that the customer address of the account code selected in cell E5 should be displayed in merged cell B6:B8.

Just in case you don't want cell B6:B8 to display a **#N/A** error value when cell E5 is empty, you can use the "IF" & "ISBLANK" with the INDEX MATCH function as follows

=IF(ISBLANK(E5),"",INDEX(Customeraddress,MATCH(E5,Customeraccount,0)))   or

=IF(E5="","",INDEX(Customeraddress,MATCH(E5,Customeraccount,0)))

Which basically means that; if cell E5 is empty, put nothing (denoted by the "" in the formula) on the merged cell B6:B8, otherwise if there is a value in cell E5, the customer address of the account code selected in cell E5 should be displayed in merged cell B6:B8. That's all it says.

Here is another example but this time we are going to return "Product description" for our lookup value and we are still using our invoice we created earlier on.

Now, select cell B11 from the invoice template and write this INDEX MATCH formula - =INDEX(Productdescription,MATCH(A11,itemcode,0)) and press enter – see figure below

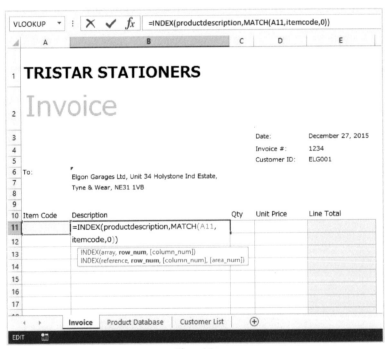

Fig. 46

You will realise that when you "Entered" there was a #N/A error value on cell B11, this is because cell A11 – your look up value is empty. To eliminate this error, Nest the INDEX MATCH formula in the "IF" & "ISBLANK" functions as explained earlier on so that your formula, will now look like this:

=IF(ISBLANK(A11),"",INDEX(Productdescription,MATCH(A11,itemcode,0))).

To make sure you really get it, now use the INDEX MATCH function to return the unit price.

And now, click the drop down arrow on cell A11, and select any item code and say for example you want to sell 4 units of that item, put 4 on cell C11 and you will see the line total on cell E11. Go ahead do it.

That was using INDEX on a one way look up.

Okay, let's take the INDEX MATCH formula a level high by looking how it does it on a 2 way lookup.

We have a range of data here showing the commissions that sales employees of a fictitious VW dealership get. Write up this data on to an excel spreadsheet starting at cell A2.

Car name/Qty	1	3	5	8	12
VW Polo	10%	12.5%	15%	17.5%	20%
VW Golf	11%	13.5%	16%	18.5%	21%
VWGolf SV	12%	14.5%	17%	19.5%	22%
VW Jetta	13%	15.5%	18%	20.5%	23%
VW Passat	14%	16.5%	19%	21.5%	24%
VW Scirocco	15%	17.5%	20%	22.5%	25%
VW Sharan	16%	18.5%	21%	23.5%	26%

Car name	VW Passat	
Qty sold	4	
Sales commission %		

Your excel worksheet should look something like fig. 47.

39

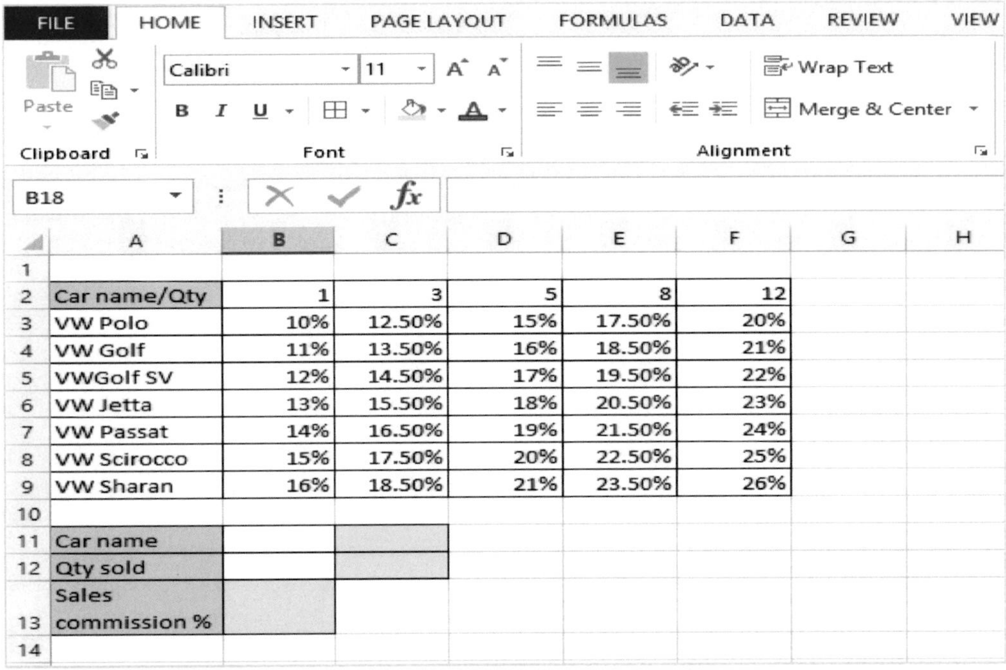

Fig. 47

Now, put a data validation for the list of car names on to cell B11(you learnt how to do this earlier on in this manual – see figure 29-34).

Select cell A3:A9 and name it *Carname*, do the same thing for cells B3:F9 and name the range *percentagecommission*, and yet again select cell B2:F2 and name it *qtysold*.

What we are essentially going to do is to find out what the sales commission would be (result in cell B13) for the number of cars sold (cell B12) of car type chosen in cell B11.

Here is a scenario;

Let's assume 6 VW Passats were sold and you want to find out what commission did the salesman get.

Here is what to do;

Select VW Passat from the drop down list in cell B11.

Then, in cell C11 type in this MATCH formula: =MATCH(B11,Carname,0) and it will return the value 5 which basically means that VW Passat is on row 5 in the named range Carname – check whether this is true.

Now, type in 6 in cell B12 (Qty of Passats sold) then select cell C12 and type in this MATCH formula: =MATCH(B12,qtysold) and enter.

Notice that we did not put a 0, or 1, or -1 after the named range for the array because the formula tells us that if you know the default value (that is what the square brackets highlighted in the formula in the figure below means), you can leave out the 0,1 or the -1 and indeed we do know the default value we want – it is a 6.

	A	B	C	D	E	F	G
1							
2	Car name/Qty	1	3	5	8	12	
3	VW Polo	10%	12.50%	15%	17.50%	20%	
4	VW Golf	11%	13.50%	16%	18.50%	21%	
5	VWGolf SV	12%	14.50%	17%	19.50%	22%	
6	VW Jetta	13%	15.50%	18%	20.50%	23%	
7	VW Passat	14%	16.50%	19%	21.50%	24%	
8	VW Scirocco	15%	17.50%	20%	22.50%	25%	
9	VW Sharan	16%	18.50%	21%	23.50%	26%	
10							
11	Car name	VW Passat	5				
12	Qty sold	6	=MATCH(B12,qtysold)				
13	Sales commission %						

MATCH(lookup_value, **lookup_array**, [match_type])

Fig. 48

Now let's find out what the sales commission would be. What we have done so far is to find out what the row value is cell C11 and what the column value is – cell C12 and now we will use this two in our INDEX function. Essentially it is INDEX(MATCH,MATCH) function – One MATCH looking at the row and the other MATCH looking at the column, hence **the 2 way lookup.**

Okay, now, select cell B13 and type in =INDEX(Percentagecommission,C11,C12) and enter and you should see 19:00% on cell B13 meaning 6 Passats sold will earn the sales person 19% commission.

You can find out the commission that a sales person will get for any named car for any quantity of that car they sell by changing the values in cells B11 & B12 since you now have the formulae in place. Go ahead play around with it.

Fine.

Now let's take it yet another level and see how the INDEX MATCH function works when you want to retrieve a whole column or a whole row of values and add them.

For example, you have 4 months sales results for the cars in the dealership. You want to find out the total sales for each using INDEX MATCH function.

Here are the results:

Employee/Month	January	February	March	April
John Fraser	4	5	3	7
Joyce Antione	3	5	7	2
Martha Tomlinson	10	1	5	8
Solomon Kish	8	4	9	1
John Darling	6	2	7	5
Tim Cameroon	1	7	3	9
Sharon Diamond	4	4	3	7

Fig. 49

Now, in your excel workbook that contains the invoice, product List, Customer list etc. open a new sheet and name it Car sales results.

Duplicate the above table in that excel worksheet starting at A3 i.e. – Employee/Month should be at A3 and at A1 put the title as Car Sales results from January to April and format it as a title.

Here is so far how your work should look:

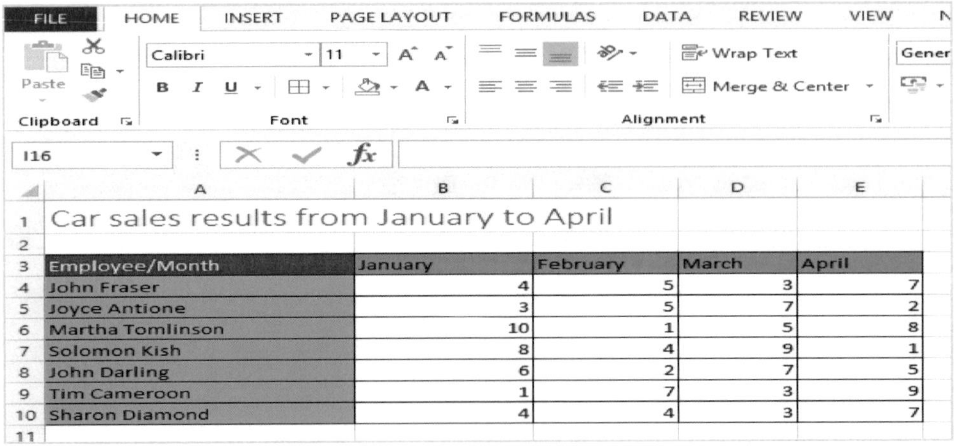

Fig. 50

Now, select cell A4:A10 and name that range *salesperson,* likewise select cell B3:E3 and name it *salesmonths,* and finally, select cells B4:E10 and name that range – *carsales.* We will use this range names later in our function, just remember them.

Okay,

Now, in cell A13, type in: "Total sales in the period by" and in cell B13 put a data validation for the whole list of the sales persons.

In cell A15 type in "Overall sales in the month of" then in cell B15 put a data validation for the list of all the sales months in the period.

In cell C12, type in the word "Result".

Now put borders in cell A13:C13 and also A15:C15 and fill cell A13 & A15 with an orange colour and cell C13 & C15 with a light grey colour.

This is how your worksheet should look like now before we put the formulae.

	A	B	C	D	E	F	G
1	Car sales results from January to April						
2							
3	Employee/Month	January	February	March	April		
4	John Fraser	4	5	3	7		
5	Joyce Antione	3	5	7	2		
6	Martha Tomlinson	10	1	5	8		
7	Solomon Kish	8	4	9	1		
8	John Darling	6	2	7	5		
9	Tim Cameroon	1	7	3	9		
10	Sharon Diamond	4	4	3	7		
11							
12			Result				
13	Total sales in the period by	▼					
14							
15	Overall Sales in the month of						
16							
17							
18							
19							
20							
21							
22							
23							

◄ ► ... | Product Database | Customer List | Car percentage sales commission | **Car sales results**

READY

Fig. 51

Okay,

You are now going to use INDEX, MATCH and SUM to retrieve a whole row of values and add them.

Here is how to do it,

Click the drop down arrow in cell B13 and for example, select Sharon Diamond from the drop down list. Thereafter, select cell C13 and type in this formula: =SUM(INDEX(carsales,MATCH(B13,salesperson,0),))

Let me explain what is going on here by explaining this formula using its constituent parts.

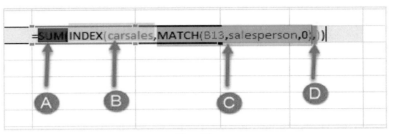

Fig. 51

By typing the above formula into cell C13, this is essentially what you are saying,

A – You are going to add all the values that

B - the INDEX function will return based on the car sales

C - of the sales person selected in B13 for the

D – whole period (all the months – the whole row).

Of course if there is no sales person yet selected at B13, the formula will return a #N/A error and to avid that, just in case you want your sheet to look neat if it is not being used, put the IF function as shown below in to cell C12 and remember to put another bracket at the end

=IF(B13="","",SUM(INDEX(carsales,MATCH(B13,salesperson,0),)))

That's one part done.

The next bit is to yet again use INDEX, MATCH and SUM to retrieve a whole column of values and add them.

Here is what you are going to do:

Click the drop down arrow in cell B15 and from the drop down list, select for example April.

Now, select cell C15 and type in this formula: =SUM(INDEX(carsales,,MATCH(B15,salesmonths,0)))

Let me explain what is going on here with this formula in relation to what we are trying to achieve – see figure below.

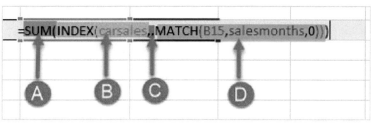

Fig. 52

What you are trying to do here is;

A – Sum up all the values

B – that the index returns from car sales

C – but not from the row (hence the [,,] sign - meaning, jump the row values) but specifically get

D – those sales values from the column that matches the sales month selected in cell B15.

There you have it.

And…

Just in case you want your sheet to look neat if it is not being used, put the IF function as shown below in to cell C15 and remember to put another bracket at the end

=IF(B15="","",SUM(INDEX(carsales,,MATCH(B15,salesmonths,0))))

A smile is my style

OTHER BOOKS BY STERLING LIBS

S NO.	BOOK TITLE
1	**THE TRAINEE ACCOUNTANT** - How to have a successful accounting career
2	**MONTH END ACCOUNTING PROCEDURES** - Detailed step by step guide
3	**THE ACCOUNTS ASSISTANT JOB MANUAL** - How to do the regular day to day tasks of an accounts assistant
4	**THE WAY TO GET AN ACCOUNTING JOB IN THE UK** - The 5 Strategic steps
5	**GET YOUR VAT RETURN DONE IN 5 STEPS**
6	**BUSINESS INTELLIGENCE** - Start, Build & Run your own business and become financially independent
7	**FINANCIAL ACCOUNTING** - UK Proctical Work Experience.
8	**HOW TO PRODUCE MANAGEMENT ACCOUNTING REPORTS –** Cash Flow Forecast, Profit & Loss, Budgets & variance analysis, break-even, KPI analysis. Work Experience guide.
9	**HOW TO FILE ACCOUNTS & ANNUAL RETURN TO HMRC & COMPANIES' HOUSE** - Detailed step by step practical experience guide for Accountants.
10	**ADVANCED EXCEL FOR ACCOUNTANTS - PIVOT TABLES & VLOOKUP** - The accountants guide to mastering pivot tables & VLOOKUP
11	**PIVOT TABLES PRACTICAL EXPERIENCE GUIDE** – Pivot tables simply & beautifully illustrated with screenshots. Accountants Edition.

HOW TO GET THESE BOOKS

1. Go to www.sterlinglibs.com or

2. Go to amazon.co.uk

3. Type in Sterling Libs at the search bar in amazon.co.uk website

4. You will see all of the above books

5. Select the one(s) you like & proceed to check out